1 3 5 7 9 10 8 6 4 2

BBC Books, an imprint of Ebury Publishing
20 Vauxhall Bridge Road,
London SW1V 2SA

BBC Books is part of the Penguin Random House group of companies
whose addresses can be found at global.penguinrandomhouse.com

Penguin
Random House
UK

First published by BBC Books in 2015

www.eburypublishing.co.uk

A CIP catalogue record for this book is available from the British Library

ISBN 9781849909686

Commissioning editor: Lorna Russell
Project editor: Charlotte Macdonald
Design: Amazing15
All images © Shutterstock

Colour origination by Amazing15
Printed and bound in Italy by Printer Trento

Penguin Random House is committed to a sustainable future for our
business, our readers and our planet. This book is made from
Forest Stewardship Council® certified paper.

TopGear

PLANET GARAGE

RICHARD PORTER

BBC
BOOKS

CONTENTS

INTRODUCTION

The garage is a bedrock of British life. Indeed, a recent survey found that the average person possesses just over 1.8 garages, although this result may have been skewed by TV's James May who owns over 50,000 of them which he keeps inside one enormous garage on a disused airbase in East Anglia.

Nonetheless, there can't be a person among us who hasn't owned a garage, seen a garage, thought about a garage or perhaps just walked into a garage. And then gone out of the garage again. Unless you're reading this in a garage, in which case you are yet to do that last part, and we salute your literalness.*

This book celebrates the garage in all of its forms. More than that, it pays tribute to all the marvellous things that can happen inside an ordinary garage. We should never forget that garage is a place where vital things are stashed, where wondrous ideas are developed, where world saving creations are brought to life, and where great thinkers of our time may gather and ruminate. You can also use it to store your car.

* Although please exercise more caution if you decide to read a book about deep sea diving. Or arson.

TYPES OF GARAGE

There are many sizes and shapes of garage but these are the most common basic types.

FREE-STANDING

The free-standing garage comes with its own four walls and its own roof. If it doesn't, something has gone badly wrong. On the plus side, this type of garage affords greater privacy and permits the garage occupant to make a wider range of loud noises – eg hammering, sawing, drumming, shouting 'OUCH' – than if the garage was attached or integral to a house. On the downside, during winter time a free-standing garage might be colder than one built into a house, and it's a longer walk back to the kitchen if you need to get milk or ask someone to find the plasters again.

ATTACHED

This type of garage is called 'attached' because it is usually attached to a house. If it is attached to something else, such as a horse or an aircraft carrier, you may want to have a serious think about what you're going to use your garage for, and also how much you want to trust the estate agent in future. The benefits of a garage that is attached to your house is that it's easier to 'pop in' to your garage at a moment's notice, possibly without even needing to put on some shoes. It's also warmer in cold weather, especially since there's a good chance your boiler lives in there. On the downside, your house may be in peril if there's an explosion or one of the animals escapes.

THE DEDICATED GARAGE DEVELOPMENT

T he dedicated garage development is a familiar sight in many towns and cities, usually in the form of identical units attached together in a long row, possibly facing an identical row to form a neat little garage village. This sort of garage is excellent for anyone who doesn't want to be bothered by their family whilst engaged in important garage business since the garage itself is almost certainly some distance from your house. Likewise, it's to the benefit of the enthusiastic garagist's family since they won't be disturbed by whatever project you're working on and the inevitable banging, clattering and sudden palls of smoke. The disadvantages of this sort of garage are that it's not next to your house, which potentially means a long walk and/or drive to get home for dinner. Also, this type of garage is quite sinister. Indeed, according to statistics we've just made up, over 70 per cent of garages in dedicated developments have been the scene of some kind of crime, especially involving Cockneys who may refer to their garage as a 'lock up'. Something to reflect if you honestly just want to store old furniture or have another go at fixing the engine of your Austin Healey Sprite.

SLOWLY ORBITING

The slowly orbiting garage is unique in that it is not attached to the ground and instead gently passes through the thermosphere, many miles above the earth. The main thing to remember about this type of garage is that it does not exist and if you start to believe that this is the type of garage you own and in which you are now standing there is every chance that somewhere within your garage the top has come off a bottle of strong cleaning chemicals and is making your brain go all strange. You should immediately step outside for some fresh air. Don't worry, you won't float off into deep space. Not unless there's a sudden and unprecedented problem with the earth's gravity, centred on a cul-de-sac in Chichester.

HOBBIES

Garages are a good place to do hobbies. That way you don't bother other people with them.

MODEL RAILWAYS

A garage is the ideal place to lay out an enormous model railway set, and many people do just that as they live out their childhood fantasy of being a train driver. Except, you're not being a train driver now, are you? To do that you'd have to be 3mm tall. What you're actually doing is living the miniaturised life of a railway infrastructure supervisor. In essence, you're doing a very boring and procedural job, but in miniature. You might as well be a tiny loss adjustor. Or a 1:76 scale model of an income-tax consultant.

SLOT RACING CARS

It's acceptable for a grown man to pretend he's driving trains around all day. If he chooses to have a massive Scalextric track in his garage, however, he might seem like a loony, even though it's probably much more exciting to zizz a little model of an Audi R18 or a Ford Escort Mexico about the place. The problem is, unless you have a friend with you, you're basically just doing a two-person pastime on your own, and that's what is strange about it. It's like playing snooker on your own. It doesn't work. Unlike model railways, which can be played with alone all day long since trains don't get into races. Perhaps, on reflection, they should.

SMOKING A PIPE

Smoking a pipe is a great lost art. Just look how mannish and clever gentlemen look in photographs from the 1940s and '50s. Why is that? It's because they're smoking pipes. Now is the time for you to adopt that practise, and where better to start than with some quality pipe time in the privacy of your own garage?

But wait: certain people – eg highly qualified doctors – now say that smoking tobacco is bad for you. But that's no problem for the amateur pipeist because you can simply clamp the pipe in your mouth without actually filling it or lighting it. Hey presto, all the benefits of smoking a pipe – eg looking clever, thoughtful, dynamic etc – with none of the downsides – eg developing emphysema, dying etc. You may want to build on the superb period charm of having a pipe in your mouth by practising classic pipe smokers' moves such as removing it from between your lips and using it to point at something, or even someone, perhaps while firmly intoning the words 'Now, look here...' Why not go the whole hog by having a drawing board installed in your office upon which you can create fascinating blueprints whilst pretending to smoke your pipe? Do this for long enough and when they finally come to take you away to the loony bin you can shout, 'Now look here! I'm in the middle of designing a supersonic airliner!' and that's sure to reassure everyone that it really is time for you to be sectioned. So, to sum up, pipe smoking is probably best avoided unless you find yourself in the actual 1950s.

HOROLOGY

Nothing is more fascinating for the keen minded chap than the workings of an old clock and the garage is the ideal place in which to dismantle such a thing without fear of a small child rampaging in and eating one of the tiny cogs. Conversely, there are inherent risks in such an endeavour, such as watching a microscopic spring flying out of the mechanism and disappearing into a pile of old plant pots or under the malfunctioning Austin Mini Traveller you keep promising to 'restore' just as soon as you've got all these bloody clocks working.

Not sure where this bit goes

BREWING BEER

The garage makes the perfect place in which to brew your own beer, firstly because it afford you some privacy in which to get on with the task in hand. Secondly, because it stops other members of the household complaining about the smell and/or leakage. And thirdly, because it minimises the risk of destroying your house if something goes badly wrong and there's an explosion. In order to brew your own beer there are several things you have to bear in mind. You must have the right equipment, you must take care to use all ingredients in carefully measured quantities, and you must at no point remember that you can buy beer in shops and it will be a lot nicer than the stuff you're making, which will have the smell, taste and strength of the stuff they use to strip the paint off submarines.

STARING WISTFULLY AT A MAP

Getting lost in thought whilst looking at a map is a noble and surprisingly time-consuming hobby. As you stare at the map, things running through your mind may include, 'Isn't the world a big place', 'look at all the places I could travel to' and 'I'm glad I'm not in any of those places right now because it's nice and warm in the garage and I've got a cup of tea on the go.'

Part 1

THE GARAGE THROUGH HISTORY

The garage has a long and interesting history (that we've just made up). Here is some of it.

merde

1809

Following victory at the Battle of Wagram, Napoleon Bonaparte instructs his deputies to invent a new type of building in which he can store his horse and which is snazzier than a common stable. The garage is born.

1810

Napoleon returns from annexing the Kingdom of Holland and is furious to discover that he can't get his horse into his new horse-storage building because some idiot has filled it with old paint tins, step ladders and that dining table he didn't need any more but which he couldn't bear to throw away.

1837

Queen Victoria accedes to the throne and becomes the first British monarch to make their official home in Buckingham Palace, which boasts the country's largest collection of garages. This is a boon for the new queen as during her time as heiress presumptive she has amassed a simply enormous number of dust sheets.

1865

Abraham Lincoln is assassinated whilst at the theatre. This is particularly annoying for the incumbent president as he hadn't wanted to watch a play that evening and was intending to sneak off into his garage to dismantle the mechanism from an old clock.

1876

Alexander Graham Bell makes the world's first telephone call to his assistant Thomas Watson and intones the words, 'Mr Watson, come here. I want to see you.' Unfortunately Watson did not hear the phone ringing as he was in his garage at the time rummaging through a large metal tin of old screws and washers.

1886

Karl Benz announces his Patent Motorwagen, the first purpose-designed and commercially available car. This is a significant landmark in the history of the garage, giving the whole idea a renewed sense of purpose. Unfortunately, Herr Benz was unable to use his own garage to store his personal Motorwagen since it was taken up with a broken table tennis table and two packing cases full of old plates.

1894

Oscar Wilde completes the first draft of his latest work, *The Importance Of Being Earnest*, which contains a hilarious reference to a garage. Unfortunately Wilde then remembers that, due to a quirk of Victorian law, it is illegal to mention garages or garage-related matters in a theatre and he changes the word 'garage' to the rather less interesting word 'handbag'.

CHOOSING A HOUSE

As everyone knows, the most important factor when buying a house is, what sort of garage does it have? Here is a brief guide to what sort of garage you can expect depending on the style of house.

GEORGIAN

The Georgians did not build garages with their houses, largely on account of it being mostly the 18th century. The idiots.

VICTORIAN

The Victorians constructed many buildings of great grandeur and pomp, but not one of them had a garage and nor did their houses. The daft wazzocks.

EDWARDIAN

Houses from this early-20th century era have many plus points But do they have garages? No. In general they do not. Avoid.

INTER-WAR

Ah, now we're getting somewhere. Many inter-war houses DID come with garages. But they were often only big enough for an Austin 7. Ergo, you can do better.

1950s & '60s

An increasingly promising period for garages which got more spacious and therefore excellent, even if some of the houses looked horrid.

1970s

Now we're really getting somewhere. 1970s houses often have massive garages. Indeed, this was the era in which the double garage became more commonplace. SUPERB.

1980s ONWARDS

Much garagey goodness can be found in houses built from the 1980s to the present day. But no more than you might get from a '70s house, and if you buy one of them you can set off the Seventiesness to a tee by purchasing an Aston Martin Lagonda to go in it. And then, on account of an untraceable electrical malfunction, never come out of it again.

Jeremy Clarkson
WHAT'S IN MY GARAGE

Hammers
(various)

Broken things
(various)

An bicycle
(please do not tell anyone about this)

NOISE

WHISTLING

W histling is something of a lost art, largely amongst men since for some reason women are rarely interested in it. The garage makes a fine place in which to recapture some of the joy of having a damn good whistle, chiefly because no one else can hear you.

CLEARING YOUR THROAT LIKE SIR TOM JONES

Sir Tom Jones is famous for three things. One, singing. Two, endlessly mentioning that he knew Elvis Presley in a way that tries to be casual whilst actually being as forced as walking around wearing a neon sign that says 'I KNEW ELVIS'. And three, clearing his throat. It's pointless attempting to replicate the first two unless you're a really good singer and/or also used to know Elvis Presley, in which case why not go over to Sir Tom Jones's house and mention this. It'll really suck the wind out of his sails. Anyway, the best way for most people to feel a bit like Sir Tom Jones is by clearing their throat in a loud and satisfying way. Unfortunately, if you attempt this in your house, on a train or in a crowded lift it might be met with great disapproval. On your own in your garage, on the other hand, there's no one to stop you. Plus, with the natural reverb that the average garage boasts, it'll sound great. If there's definitely no one listening you might want to follow up the throat clearing by loudly going 'HOUGH!' like Sir Tom Jones does on that record. Or just shouting, 'I knew Elvis you know!' like Sir Tom Jones does in every single interview.

DRUMMING

Playing drums falls into two camps. If you're good at it, it's an impressive delight to behold. If you're not, it's ghastly and unpleasant for all concerned. In this respect, it's rather like heart surgery or landing a plane. Except that, unlike those things, playing the drums can be done in your garage without causing more problems than it solves. More than that, the garage is the ideal place in which to drum because there's less chance of annoying others with your flailing, off-tempo racket or visitors asking if somewhere in your house there is an angry, arrhythmic monkey.

I knew Elvis

To ensure maximum comfort for others, why not crudely soundproof your garage by taping egg boxes to the walls. Just remember to take out the eggs first. Otherwise there will be mess and a smell. Even more so than normal where drummers are concerned.

GARAGE MUSIC

There are several types of music that have garage in the title. These are them. Or they. Or is it those? Erm…

1960S GARAGE

An American music genre and the most authentically garagey since its name comes from bands rehearsing in actual garages. This can be seen in some of the song titles of garage bands such as 'Cans Of Half Used Paint', 'Hey! Has Your Family Got A New Boiler?' and 'Woah! Dad! Don't Drive In Here, We're Rehearsing (Oh God, This Is SO Unfair)'. This type of garage music died out in the late '60s when Ryan's dad decided to turn the garage into a home office.

REPRESENTATIVE ARTISTS: The Busybees; Dick, Dick, Daisy & Dick; The Silly; Warm Garbage.

Daddy-o!

US GARAGE

As its name suggests, US garage was a type of American dance music popular in the 1980s and centred around a New York nightclub called the Paradise Garage which was not an actual garage, although it did used to be a car park. Legend has it that patrons were constantly reminded to get out of their cars before attempting to enter the club whilst signs in the lavatories reminded customers of the management's zero tolerance policy to people attempting to use the premises to store step ladders, dust sheets and a broken occasional table that they swore one day they would get around to fixing.

REPRESENTATIVE ARTISTS:

Tony Cologne; Danny Fantastically; Hot Bobby; Randy Sweat

DADDY IS GOING TO BE FURIOUS WHEN HE SEES WHAT TIMOTHY, OLIVER, SEBASTIAN AND POLLY HAVE DONE TO THE DOUBLE GARAGE

UK GARAGE

U K garage was a British phenomenon of the 1990s which could be identified by an uptempo, skittering beat, highly processed vocals and a video featuring someone titting about in front of a mid-range Mercedes. UK garage was influenced by US garage but with extra rubbishness. Its lyrics had a uniquely local flavour and often referenced specific and controversial British subjects such as buying chips, yesterday's episode of *Kilroy*, what sort of pay-as-you-go mobile to get and today's episode of *Kilroy*.

REPRESENTATIVE ARTISTS: Allnite Kebabz; Buz Shelta; Ryce & Chipz; Kilroy Watchaz

GARAGE GATES

2002 *Pop Idol* runner up and creator of teeny stammering trend, Gates later disappeared from public view after disappointed garage enthusiasts discovered he did not have a galvanised up-and-over door, could not be used to store a lawnmower and was not the ideal place in which to embark on a project to strip down the engine from an Austin Princess. Also, it turned out his name was 'Gareth' not 'garage'.

Part 2

THE GARAGE THROUGH HISTORY

Damn it! Where did I put my dinghy?

1912

Captain Edward Smith of the White Star Line announces his new invention, 'the unfillable garage'. Unfortunately, before being able to test out his concept Smith is called away to captain White Star's new flagship, RMS Titanic, on its maiden voyage. As a result, he never gets to see that once his garage has two step ladders, an old dinghy, some boxes of books and a broken armchair in it, it is by any reasonable definition 'full'.

1914

Europe is brought to the brink of war by the assassination of Archduke Franz Ferdinand of Austria. His killer, Gavrilo Princip, is actually aiming for a bottle on a wall but the shot is deflected into the Archduke's neck after ricocheting off the metal up-and-over door of a nearby garage.

1922

Jazz music sweeps the United States and many other parts of the world, helped by growing radio ownership. Jazz musicians are encouraged to play in garages, mainly because then no one else has to hear them.

ALLSTAR JAZZ LIVE MUSIC
TUESDAY NIGHTS!
BEHIND THE BINGO HALL, 3rd GARAGE ON THE LEFT

1940

Prime Minister Winston Churchill delivers his famous 'We shall fight on the beaches' speech to parliament. The great orator later admits that he inadvertently omitted the line 'we shall fight in the garages' and expresses regret at this error since 'dried-up paint brushes, folded up director's chairs and tins of screws are this country's most precious resource'.

1962

After recording at Abbey Road studios for the first time, The Beatles sack Pete Best and replace him with Ringo Starr, not because he is a better drummer but because he owns a small garage and has promised to let John Lennon use it to store a small table, a box of saucepans and an enormous amount of string. In 1987 the string is sold at auction for $4.7m.

1969

Man lands on the moon for the first time, a moment marked by Neil Armstrong's famous 'One small step for man' speech. What's less widely known is that immediately after this, Armstrong sent another transmission to mission control; 'Tell Janet, it's in the drawer next to the refrigerator'. This was a response to a second-hand message Armstrong received from his wife as he approached the moon saying that she couldn't find the key to the garage.

TYPES OF GARAGE DOOR

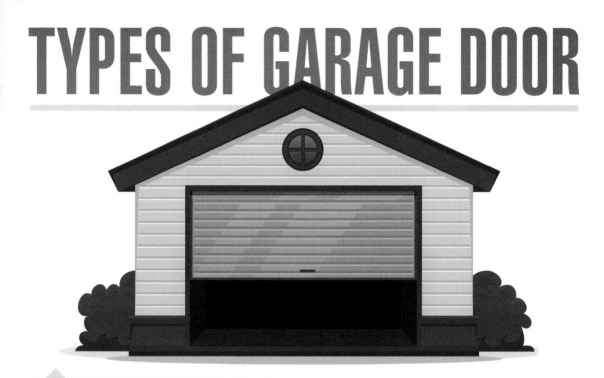

ROLLER SHUTTER

The roller shutter promises the ability to quickly reveal the contents of your garage whilst shouting 'Hey presto!' but with an added touch of industrial chic. Not that most garages need such a thing. In fact, the down side of the roller shutter is that it makes your garage look a bit too much like a small industrial unit which in turn makes it seem suspicious, leading your neighbours to assume you are deeply involved in the manufacture and/or distribution of drugs.

UP-AND-OVER

The classic garage door of the modern era, the up-and-over has several advantages. It's quick, it's simple, it gives the opportunity to sling it open with all your might whilst shouting 'ta-daaaa' (should the need arise). On the downside, it's a bit noisy and if one of the supports breaks during operation you will receive a sudden and unwelcome reminder that metal garage doors are quite heavy.

AUTOMATIC UP-AND-OVER

Combining all the smooth, simple convenience of the traditional up-and-over with all the lazy benefits of electrical power, the automatic up-and-over is increasingly popular amongst people who literally can't be bothered to get out of their cars or who like their doors, where possible, to start opening whilst they are still some distance away. The main downside of the automatic up-and-over is that inevitably at some point you will become consumed with a desire to pretend you are Indiana Jones and set the door closing before attempting to roll underneath it. This will end in one of two ways; satisfyingly. Or very, very embarrassingly.

SIDE-HINGED

A classic in the world of garage doors. Not the fastest or the most modern, but steeped in a great sense of occasion as you carefully swing back each door in turn, proudly revealing all those boxes you've never got round to unpacking since you moved in seven years ago or that partially dismantled Triumph Stag that you have no idea how to reassemble. On the downside, the side-hinged system tends to feature doors made of wood which will inevitably go a bit rotten at the bottom. Also, it's quite common for the hinges to drop so that one or both doors scrape along the ground and have to be held up as they're moved in a way only the owner of the garage fully understands. But this is a small price to pay. Some garagists may even regard it as a bonus.

SLIDING DOORS

The sideways slide of a metal door can make the garage owner feel terribly modern, as if they are part of an Formula 1 team or a very small space programme. On the downside, the smooth and grand retraction of the door may lead passers by to expect something rather special inside, such as an F1 car or a Space Shuttle. To watch the high-tech door disappear, thereby revealing a broken standard lamp and a chest freezer is only going to lead to disappointment.

WOODWORK

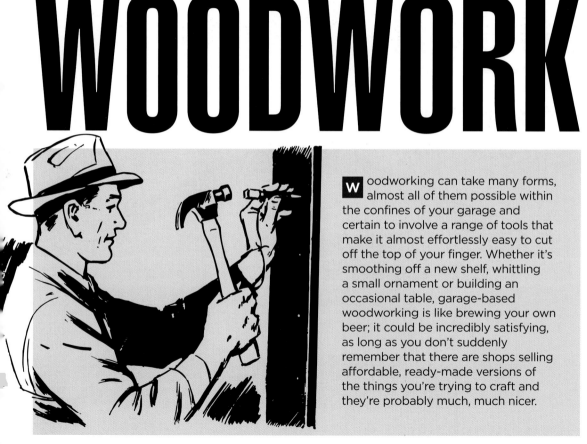

Woodworking can take many forms, almost all of them possible within the confines of your garage and certain to involve a range of tools that make it almost effortlessly easy to cut off the top of your finger. Whether it's smoothing off a new shelf, whittling a small ornament or building an occasional table, garage-based woodworking is like brewing your own beer; it could be incredibly satisfying, as long as you don't suddenly remember that there are shops selling affordable, ready-made versions of the things you're trying to craft and they're probably much, much nicer.

Richard Hammond
WHAT'S IN MY GARAGE

Manuals on how to fix a broken old Land Rover
(several)

Parts to fix a broken old Land Rover
(several)

An old Land Rover
(still broken)

PART #1

CAR IMPROVEMENT

Making your People Carrier a Convertible

STEP 1

Drive your people carrier into your garage. Remember to remove other items from the garage first such as old furniture, boxes of newspapers, or the home office you converted the garage into some six years ago.

STEP 2

Carefully mark the places on the bodywork where you are going to cut. Or just remember them using your brain. Either is good. Also, make sure the pillars you're going to cut through don't have an airbag on the other side. Remember the fuss John from next door made last time there was an almighty bang from the garage? 'Blah blah blah call an ambulance yadda yadda yadda having a heart attack' and so on. We don't want a repeat of that.

STEP 3

Cut through the base of the second, third and fourth side pillars of the car. That's counting from the front. You probably want to leave the windscreen in place. Unless you like strong breezes. Once you've done that, cut a line across the car just above the windscreen. You should probably do all this with a circular saw or similar. If you're trying it with the kitchen scissors you're going to be there all day.

STEP 4

Carefully remove the roof and pillars from the rest of the car. Wait. Your people carrier was a Renault Espace mk1, 2 or 3 with its separate chassis and non-load-bearing panels wasn't it? It wasn't? Ah, right. That's probably why your car's just snapped in half. Sorry, should have mentioned this earlier. Still, the garage will make an ideal place in which to make a panicky attempt to weld the floorpan back together.

STEP 5

Enjoy. Now is not the time to listen to the naysayers accusing you of 'completely ruining' the family car.

ANIMALS

Animals have a strong connection to the garage, depending on what sort of garage it is and other factors such as how warm it is, how big it is, and how many lions are in it.

CATS

Cats can live in a garage. However, cats are not stupid. They would rather live in the house where it is warmer and there is more food. Ergo, if you attempt to make a cat live in the garage the cat will find a way to move into the house and, if left unchecked, one day you will wake up to discover that now you live in the garage whilst the cat has the house, and now the cat has changed all the locks and redecorated the sitting room in a most peculiar way. On that basis, it's best just to let the cat in the house from day one.

PREVENTING YOUR FAMILY FROM DISCOVERING THAT PANDA YOU BOUGHT OFF EBAY BY MISTAKE

The garage could be the ideal place to store the panda that you bought off eBay by accident, especially if you don't want your family to know what you've done. Just remember to keep the panda well fed and watered and with a stack of magazines to read. It's also vital that if you don't want your family to know about this, you must keep them out of the garage at all times. This can be achieved by relatively simple means such as saying, 'Do not go into the garage children, there is a very angry bear in there.' Under NO circumstances should you say, 'Do not go into the garage because there is a panda in there.' Everyone will only want to go and look at the panda, after which they may have some salient questions such as 'Dad, why is there a panda in our garage?' and you'll have to explain how you bought it by accident from eBay because you failed to spot the difference between the word 'Fiat' and the words 'an actual live'.

HOW TO TELL IF SOMEONE IS SECRETLY KEEPING A PANDA IN YOUR GARAGE

- Keep disappearing into the garage with armfuls of bamboo
- Appear to have taken out subscription to panda-interest magazine
- Panda noises

GOOSE STORAGE

We've all been there. You've got far too many geese and you just don't know what to do with them all. Well, have you considered storing them in your garage? It could be the ideal place to stash an goose or geese, especially if you also use your garage to stash items of value. As everyone knows, geese are vicious sods and will deter anyone from entering your garage, including you. It's a goose garage now. Let it go.

BOILERS

Boilers are mammals. They are carnivorous and have long muscular tails. If you find a boiler in your garage, please take it immediately to a local river and put it into the water.
CORRECTION: It appears the word 'boiler' was wrongly used in this section of the book in place of the correct word which is 'otter'.

THE GARAGE WEASEL

A creature ideally suited to living in and around a garage, the garage weasel's diet consisted largely of old newspapers, dried up paint, and small boxes of fuses that no one was ever going to use. Ironically, the garage weasel got its name for entirely different reasons and became extinct two years before the garage was invented.

METALWORK

Metalworking ideally requires a lathe and the garage is the ideal place to have one installed. There is little in the world to match the manly feeling of confidently operating a lathe, except perhaps chopping logs whilst smoking a pipe. But let's not be sexist here, because women can use a lathe too. It's just that, on average, they choose not to. Nonetheless, in 1957 Babcocks of Preston introduced a radical 'Lady Lathe' to their range and according to the official brochure, it boasted an 'attractive pink paint job' and a 'lady-like headstock and spindle' that would 'make your lass look right super as she spot faces a cylinder head and that'. Of course these days it's all done on computers or something.

COMPANIES FOUN

Many of the world's biggest and best known companies were actually founded in the humble garage. Here is a list of famous names that genuinely got their start in a garage. Some of the other facts on this page might be wrong.

AMAZON

The company's founders decided to establish the company one afternoon and were amazed that it turned up by the middle of the next morning.

APPLE

You know what it's like; you pop out to the garage to look for string, accidentally come back with the world's most valuable computing giant.

DED IN A GARAGE

DISNEY

Next time you see a mouse in your garage, don't set the cat on it. Use it as the basis for a character that will found a vast media empire.

GOOGLE

You're searching for 'wasy to fuond a cpomny ina gragare' Did you mean 'ways to found a company in a garage'?

HARLEY DAVIDSON

The 'bike maker was founded in the low key surroundings of a garage. Shortly after this the garage had a crisis, grew a pony tail, and ran off with a shed half its age.

HEWLETT-PACKARD

The massive electronic hardware company was founded in a garage in the small American town of Paper Jam.

LOTUS

Colin Chapman came up with his first sports car in a garage, little knowing that many of his subsequent models would also end up there.

MICROSOFT

"I see that your trying to start a global software giant in your garage! Can I help with that?"

STARTING YOUR OWN COMPANY IN YOUR GARAGE

The garage is a great place to start a business. However, this requires planning and dedication. Here are a few tips to bear in mind.

(£) Have you really got nowhere in the house where you could stick a desk? Garages are quite draughty and often smell of turps. Is this the best environment in which to work or will you get giddy off the fumes and accidentally set up a business that sells towels to giraffes?

(£) How are you going to make your garage look more business-like? Remember, you may have to bring potential investors here to discuss important things. If you greet them outside and ask them to 'step into the garage' they may assume your intention is to extort money out of them by attacking them with a large spanner or painty piece of wood.

(£) Office layout is very important. It's no good having inspiringly businessy pictures of nocturnal cityscapes like the reception area on *The Apprentice* if they're attached to the inside of the garage door. Someone is only going to open it by accident and they'll all fall on the floor. This does NOT happen to Lord Sir Sugar. At least, not that we've seen.

£ If the garage is your office, consider bolting shut the garage door. Otherwise you'll be right in the middle of a vital meeting with a high profile client when one wall of your office will fly open and you'll both get run over by a car.

£ Once you've thought of a name you can then make it seem more intriguing and sinister by adding the word 'industries' to the end. Compare and contrast:

Petticoat Meadow Ltd
Petticoat Meadow Industries Ltd

See!

£ Speaking of names, consider giving your garage a new and more dynamic name to be used on all business postal correspondence. 'The Optimal Centre' or 'Power Zone' or something like that. Just think, what would Sir Alan Sugar Lord do? Well, he'd probably call it The Lord Alan Sir Sugar Centre. Don't call your garage that. It's stupid.

IN

A fter that, it's all up to you and your fledgling business-in-the-garage idea. Just one piece of advice; don't copy anything you see on *The Apprentice*. Otherwise you'll waste ten weeks sitting in your garage squawking on about '110 per cent' and 'the process' before realising you have confused the idea of running an actual business with the idea of being a power suited buffoon with less business acumen than a moderately bright five-year-old. At which point, thank your garage for the opportunity, grab a small wheelie suitcase, walk outside into a cab and sod off.

PART #2

CAR IMPROVEMENT

THE AFFORDABLE ELECTRIC CAR

Electric cars are increasingly fashionable but they're also expensive. Here's how to make one in your garage for a fraction of the cost.

Owners Garage Manual

STEP 1: Get a separate chassis from a car that has a separate chassis, eg an TVR.

STEP 2: Remove the petrol engine from the chassis and replace it with an electric motor from an milkfloat.

TOP GEAR: **PLANET GARAGE**

STEP 3:

At the other end of the chassis add a lot of car batteries. No really, A LOT. You can't have too many. Oh wait. Are you wearing rubber gloves? You probably should be wearing rubber gloves for this one, what with all the electricity and stuff. Sorry, should have mentioned that earlier.

STEP 4:

Clothe the new engine, battery and chassis combo in a hand made, super lightweight aluminium body held together with the metal strakes from a cheap shelving unit.

STEP 5:

Hey presto! Yes, yes, yes, it looks terrible. But don't worry, the range is so poor and the on-board power unit so noxious you won't be able to drive anywhere in it anyway. Problem solved!

GARAGE APPS

The garage has come roaring into the modern world and there are now several apps that can help you with your garageing.

WHERE'S MY GARAGE?

This handy app instantly tells you where your garage is. Commonly returned answers include 'Attached to your house', 'Where you left it' and 'You're in it'.

WHAT'S IN MY GARAGE?

Organise your garage by ticking off items from a pre-set list which includes expected items like 'car', 'ladder' and 'old kitchen tiles' and more controversial entries such as 'stolen artworks', 'another panda' and 'the rest of the hitchhiker'.

GARAGE HAT

Talk to other garages in your area! Not entirely clear why you'd want to do that or indeed what they'd say, rendering this app idiotic and pointless.

GRAGR

Find other garages looking for a good time! Attracted controversy in 2014 when a study found over three-quarters of the participants were actually middle-aged men and not single garages at all.

GARAGE CONTROLLER

Take complete control of your garage from your smart phone. See dried-up paint levels, check number of redundant Allen keys in small plastic bag, see how many folded-up dust sheets there are thrown in the corner. Requires additional hardware and up to five months of extremely tedious auditing.

GARAGESTACHE

Take a picture of your garage and then use amazing rendering technology to see what it would look like with a moustache! Described by *Which App? Online* as 'completely pointless and in some cases upsetting'.

James May
WHAT'S IN MY GARAGE

1x Brompton folding bicycle
1x Honda Super Cub motorcycle
1x 30 piece forged steel screwdriver and bit set
1x 36 piece ¼" drive socket set
1x single phase electric lathe
1x electric kettle
1x box tea bags (current contents: 43 bags)
4x mugs (various)
1x confiscated items box
(current contents; 1x hammer marked 'Property of J. Clarkson. HANDS OFF')

GARAGES IN TV PROGRAMMES

Garages have made an appearance in many television shows. Here are some of the most famous of those.

WHAT EVER HAPPENED TO THE LIKELY LADS? (1974)

In series two of the much-loved sit-com, Bob agrees to let Terry sleep by the boiler in his garage on the understanding that they must keep this secret from Bob's wife Thelma. The episode, entitled 'Some Like It Hot', ends with Thelma brutally attacking Terry with a Hoover attachment. The programme was never broadcast, not because of this bloody and frenzied assault but because it was deemed to contain an unacceptable amount of skiffle music.

AIRWOLF (1985)

In this controversial episode of the popular 1980s helicopter shenanigans show, Stringfellow Hawke and Dominic Santini are forced to move out of their secret underground cave base because it is being redecorated and must stash their precious ultrachopper in the garage of Santini's Los Angeles home so that the CIA don't come and steal it. Unfortunately, during this endeavour Hawke is taking powerful medicine to clear up a septic ear and this causes him to start up Airwolf, forgetting that it is in a confined space. As a result, the rotor blades snap off and a pile of old newspapers is blown over. This episode was described by fans as 'stupid and boring'.

BERGERAC (1989)

In an episode entitled '*Garage de mystère*' eponymous hero Jim Bergerac becomes convinced that some stolen jewels have been stashed in a free-standing garage behind a hotel and spends most of the episode rampaging about trying to discover who has the keys to the up-and-over door. It's only towards the end of his deranged quest that he realises the garage isn't actually locked and triumphantly flings open the door to reveal its contents are not illicit diamonds but a broken bicycle and half a Hillman Imp. Amongst *Bergerac* fans this episode is also known as 'the one where Bergerac started drinking again'.

SEX AND THE CITY (1999)

The four girls are told that the very latest Jimmy Choo shoes are going on display in 'the garage' that very afternoon and they abandon plans for lunch in order to check them out. Unfortunately, a mix up sees them go into in an actual garage rather than fashionable uptown shop The Garage and instead of spending the episode in a restaurant talking vacuous drivel about clothes and penises, they are forced to sit in an empty garage talking vacuous drivel about clothes and penises.

FRIENDS (2001)

At the start of this episode of the smash hit sit-com, David Schwimmer's character thinks he sees an ex-girlfriend entering an abandoned garage and walks in only for the door to slam shut, trapping him inside on his own. He is not seen for the rest of the episode. This particular programme was created in response to audience research which said that viewers found Ross an incredibly annoying character and wished he wasn't on the show. The episode was even referred to as 'The One Where Ross Only Appears Briefly At The Beginning Then Gets Locked In A Garage And Doesn't Feature At All In The Rest Of The Show, Thank God'.

DOCTOR WHO (2006)

With the TARDIS in for a service, The Doctor is at a loose end until he meets a chap called Barry who says the can use his garage in Ipswich. It's only later that the Doctor realises Barry is a delusional lunatic and his garage is not capable of travelling through space and time. Fans were not impressed with this episode when it aired since it largely involved Doctor Who standing in a garage in Ipswich looking a bit irritable.

POLICE PUBLIC CALL BOX

POLICE TELEPHONE
FREE
FOR USE OF
PUBLIC
ADVICE & ASSISTANCE
OBTAINABLE IMMEDIATELY
OFFICERS & CARS
RESPOND TO ALL CALLS
PULL TO OPEN

ST JOHN AMBULANCE

JOURNEY TO THE CENTRE OF THE G.A.R.A.G.E.

WELDING

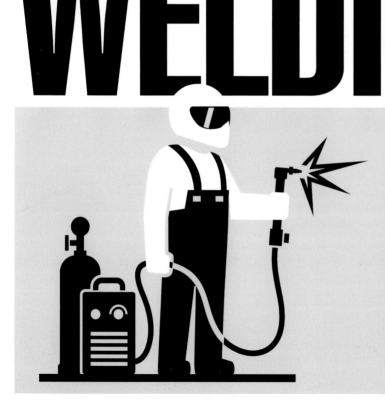

Welding comes in many forms. There's TIG and MIG and also the little know STIG welding, in which two metal items are joined together using seagull residue and the power of the mind. All of them requiring at least a modicum of skill. In the right hands, welding can be fantastically satisfying, constructive and useful. In the wrong hands, which is most of them, it's just a tremendously good way to set your garage on fire.

NAMING YOUR GARAGE

You don't have to name your garage. In fact, on reflection, it's an idiotic idea. But if you insist, here are some suggestions.

- EL PONDEROSA
- SHAKATAK
- LE GARAGE
- THE BADGER'S NEST
- EL GARAGEO
- THE PANDAERY
- STEVE'S GARAGE*

MAN CAVE

You should resist giving this name to your garage. It is deeply annoying. In fact, the best response to anyone adopted a jocular expression and referring to your garage as 'a man cave' is to shout 'Oh SHUT UP Nigel'*.

THE BEST NAME FOR A GARAGE

The best way to refer to your garage is as your 'lair'. This makes it sound interesting, sinister and perhaps a bit mysterious.

- Add a question mark to the end of your name, eg Peter Harrison?
- Look at everything through narrow eyes
- Answer all questions evasively, and with another question. eg 'Where are you from?' 'I don't know. Where are YOU from?'

OTHER WAYS TO SEEM MORE MYSTERIOUS

* Names may vary

BUILDING YOUR OWN GARAGE

Many of us harbour the low-to-mid-level ambition to build our own garage. If this applies to you, there are a few things to bear in mind.

It'll be easy, darling. You might even get a shelf.

I'm leaving you.

1 Do you actually know how to build a garage? It's harder than it looks, especially if you want a roof and/or a roof that stays on.

2 Do you know what a garage is? Are you sure you're not confusing the word 'garage' with the word 'sandwich' again? In which case, stop reading this book. There are no recipes. Except in the recipe section.

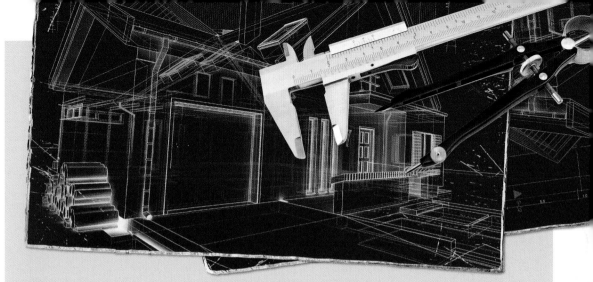

3 Do you have planning permission to construct a garage? You may read on the internet that garages do not need planning permission along with some spurious reason such as 'they are outbuildings', 'they are only quite small' or 'they are mammals'. None of these are true. Before you build you garage, a man in polyester slacks must come round and tell you it's okay.

4 Why are you building a garage? It's not to live in again is it? For God's sake Peter, when are you going to sort your life out? What? No, we haven't seen Jennifer. Well yes, last we heard she had moved in with her new chap. Peter. Peter, seriously, stop sobbing. She's moved on. And not into a garage. Look Peter, we've got to go now, we're supposed to be doing a list about garage building. Okay, bye.

5 What are you going to use your garage for? If the answer is 'tennis', 'motorsport' or 'airport' it's very possible a garage is not what you should be building on the land.

Have you got planning
permission for this?

No, but I have just
nailed my arm to
this plank.

Garages are covered by building regulations, just like any other permanent structure. Do not attempt to dodge this by claiming that you're crap at building and your garage will 'probably fall down soon'. For some reason, building inspectors do not find this sort of thing very funny.

Here are some things your garage should and shouldn't have in order to meet building regulations:

 Four walls, one of them with a big door hole in it

 A roof, preferably well attached to the walls

 Adequate drainage from roof using well specified guttering.

 Obvious and unquenchable fire occurring inside

 Machine gun nests and rotating knives

X Intricately inlaid contrast colour brickwork spelling out the words BUILDING INSPECTORS ARE IDIOTS

Interestingly, building regulations do not specify how large or small a garage has to be to qualify as a garage. However, if it's big enough to store an aircraft in that's probably not a garage as such. It's a hangar. Are you really sure you're got planning permission for this?

GARAGE HATS

WOOLLY HAT

The classic garage hat. Warm, practical, ideally dark coloured so it won't show up the stains caused by oil dripping on your head. Spending time in your garage during the period from September to April isn't the same without a woolly hat. For one thing, it's colder.

BOBBLE HAT

Comedy cousin of the stout British woolly hat boasting all the same warm, sensible values but with the added bonus of making you look a bit of a tit. No wait, that's not a bonus at all. Cut the bobble off immediately, unless you have a weekend job impersonating a Swedish tourist.

BASEBALL CAP

Is your garage in Alabama and are you in there stripping down the Hemi V8 from your Dodge Charger? If yes, the baseball cap is ideal, nay mandatory. If the answer is, 'No, I'm in Hemel Hempstead trying to get this Austin Maxi started' (or similar) a baseball cap might make you look like a berk.

Wearing a hat in the garage is a perfectly natural thing, especially since it might get a bit cold in there. Here are some of your options.

FLAT CAP

A textbook hat if you are using your garage to store an old British sports car. In fact, it is actually illegal to drive an old British sports car without wearing a flat cap, preferably in tweed. Alternatively, you can wear the hat in your garage whilst standing next to your old British sports car and reflecting on the terrible mess you seem to have made of the engine, electrics and paintwork.

FEDORA

If it's 1940 and you're in the garage making moonshine or tuning your Ford's Flathead V8 to outrun the cops before another bootlegging run across the state line into Georgia, the fedora would be a fine hat to wear. If you are not pursuing one or more of these activities – eg because you live in Macclesfield and have a Ford Mondeo diesel – then the fedora is probably not the garage hat for you.

FEZ

Superficially, this seems an odd choice of hat to wear in the garage, unless you are Tommy Cooper. But if you proudly declare it to be your 'project hat' and then only wear it when you're off to the garage, people will assume you've gone a bit mad, they will leave you alone and that means they won't discover the bloody panda.

ARE YOU TRAPPED UNDER THE AUTOMATIC DOOR OF YOUR GARAGE?

Don't Panic!

Here at JACKSON KRESP & SON we've been rescuing people from the embarrassing aftermath of their idiotic Indiana Jones impression for over 20 years!

Simply call us on 01632 960684 and we'll be on our way to set you free within three to five working days!

Remember, don't just lay there shouting 'Ahh, this is even more painful than it looks, please God, someone get help!' Just call the experts! We'll get you free in no time and we promise we'll hardly laugh at your predicament at all. Although we might take a picture and put it on our Facebook page.

Jackson Kresp & Son

Clearing up the aftermath of your stupidity since 1995!

PICTURE FRAMING

At some point in life, almost everyone needs a picture framing. At some point in life, almost everyone also finds themselves saying, 'How much?! Just to frame a picture?! Bloody hell!'. Framing a picture isn't difficult. Framing a picture and doing a good job is difficult, but if you learn this skill and turn your garage into a picture framing studio, over their lifetime the average person would save themselves up to £1 million.

CAR
IMPROVEMENT

THE AMPHIBIOUS CAR

Amphibious cars sound like a great idea yet for some reason they've never taken off. But why wait for the idle car makers of the world to finally come up with something you can buy when you could do it yourself in the garage? Here's how;

Owners Garage Manual

STEP 1

Select your car. It can be pretty much anything, although for various reasons we would strongly advise against a VW campervan and for various other reasons we would also caution against an old Triumph Herald with a sail on top, especially if you actually want to get to, or at least near, your intended destination.

STEP 2

Bolt an outboard motor to the back. The more powerful, the better.

STEP 3

Build a rudimentary hull around the lower reaches of the car.

STEP 4

Fill the engine bay, wheelarches, box sections and as much of the interior as possible with buoyancy-enhancing expanding foam. If you look at how much expanding foam is in your car and you think it's 'too much', trust us on this one, that's when the real answer is 'not enough'.

STEP 5

Drive into some water.

STEP 6

Sink.

We probably should have mentioned that last one a bit earlier. Sorry.

MORE GARAGE MUSIC

Garages have a long association with musicians and music. Here are some you might not know about.

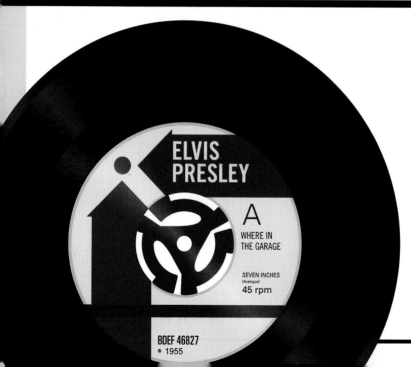

ELVIS
PRESLEY

A
WHERE IN
THE GARAGE

SEVEN INCHES
(Analogue)
45 rpm

BDEF 46827
℗ 1955

ELVIS PRESLEY

In 1955 a young singer called Elvis Presley recorded a song called 'Where In The Garage'. His record company pointed out that this otherwise excellent track was undermined by the rather boring lyrics which were mostly about trying to find a bicycle tyre pump which had become misplaced somewhere within his garage. The words were hastily changed and Presley re-recorded the song with a new title, 'Heartbreak Hotel'.

Wuzza wuzza

DAVID BOWIE

Holed up in Berlin working on what would become his masterpiece, *"Heroes"*, the artist sometimes known as The Thin White Duke found himself struggling with lyrics for the title track and in particular the couplet, 'I, I can remember / Standing, by the garage door' which Bowie and producer Tony Visconti agreed 'didn't really fit'. Bowie wracked his brain for another large structure that he could claim to have been standing next to. Then he looked out of the window and remembered that Berlin is home to a large wall. So he used that instead.

PET SHOP BOYS

The popular synthesizer duo's first hit, 'West End Girls', was originally called 'West End Garage' and was written after the quiet one rented a lock-up near Kensington High Street in order to store his Austin Maestro Vanden Plas. The words and title were later changed after he told singer Neil Tennant that he didn't want people looking for the garage and bothering him on a Sunday when he was trying to vacuum the floor mats.

TAYLOR DANE

I Taylor Dane's 1988 top ten hit 'Tell It To My Heart' was originally called 'Tell It To My Garage'. The title was changed after it was realised that this made no sense whatsoever and the garage probably wouldn't be listening.

JANET JACKSON

Popular American singer Janet Jackson was originally called Janet Garage as a result of her debut single being sponsored by a US chain of garage door fitting specialists. She later reverted back to her family name, except in Bulgaria where the name 'Janet Jackson' was already associated with a best selling brand of tractor lubricant.

Miss Garage, if you're nasty!

DURAN DURAN

T he famed new romantic five-piece started life as Garage Garage because founding members John Taylor and Andy Rhodes both had garages which they needed in order to have room in which to story their extremely puffy sleeves and vast quantities of eye liner. When singer Simon le Bon joined the group, he insisted the name was changed as he himself did not have a garage and found the whole subject rather a sore point.

Because maybe,
You're gonna be the one that saves me,
And after all,
You're my garage door

OASIS

Whilst recording their second album, lead singer Liam Gallagher suggested that to his brother Noel that a track they were working on should be called 'Garage Door'. The guitarist and songwriter described this as 'A fooking rubbish idea' and pointed out that his younger brother 'didn't even have a fooking garage'. Liam then attempted to claim he had 'a garage of the fooking mind' and the subsequent argument raged on for an incredible 17 days, after which the brothers couldn't remember what they were arguing about, put aside their differences and decided to call the song 'Wonderwall'.

TAKE THAT

The ever-shrinking former boy band almost called their first album *Take That In The Garage* after a proposed sleeve photo that showed the group looking for a set of Allen keys in Gary Barlow's garage. The lead singer later changed the title to *Take That & Party* after decreeing that the photo was outdated because he had located the Allen keys. It turned out that Kylie Minogue had borrowed them.

THE GARAGE THROUGH HISTORY

1971

American business man Robert P. McCulloch buys the old London Bridge, has it re-assembled in Arizona and is rendered furious by what he sees. His anger is popularly mis-reported as the result of his mistaken belief that he had purchased Tower Bridge not London Bridge. This is not true. McCulloch was actually cross because he thought he was buying something called 'London Garage' and without it he has nowhere to store his legendary collection of white plastic garden furniture and lawnmowers. In 1972 he solved this problem by paying $1.4m for The Leaning Shed of Pisa.

1975

The British Leyland Motor Corporation is nationalized. The vast company comprises over 50 properties, hundreds of thousands of employees, over 30 model variants in its car range alone, and a small garage in Sutton Coldfield containing a broken Austin Cambridge which it keeps promising it will get round to sorting.

1985

The wreck of the Titanic is found, over two miles beneath the surface of the Atlantic Ocean. Ironically, it is found accidentally by oceanographers looking for the legendary Atlantic Garage, a mythical structure which is said to contain unimaginable riches of green garden string and cloudy bottles of paintbrush cleaner.

Get lost!

1994

The Channel Tunnel opens much to the dismay of the French who were secretly building a vast underground garage known as *Le Garage de la Manche* and were rather put out when the British poked a tunnelling machine through the back wall.

2000

Fear of the Millennium Bug sweeps the world. Across Britain thousands of people wonder if the bug will cause the paint in those half-used cans in the garage to dry up, although in fact that happened not long after they were first put there, seven years ago.

2003

Innovative website MySpace is set up, initially as a place on which avid garage fans can log the contents of their garage and what they're doing in there. After a few months of little interest, it is re-launched as a music-based social networking site and becomes a global phenomenon, to the annoyance of its previous user base, which was two men called Nigel.

2007

Google Street View makes its debut and is almost immediately mired in controversy as a man in Lincolnshire objects to his garage being viewable around the world. Google later blurs his garage to 'respect privacy, and stop people seeing the mess he's made of that Wolseley Hornet'.

WHERE TO PUT YOUR GARAGE

**THE CLASSIC.
YOU WON'T GO FAR
WRONG WITH THIS.**

IT'S BRAVE BUT MAY LEAD TO IMPRACTICALITY AND DRAUGHTS.

INNOVATIVE, YES. BUT ALSO RATHER INCONVENIENT, ESPECIALLY IF THERE'S AN LOTUS ECLAT IN THERE ALREADY.

WELL THAT'S JUST STUPID.
WHAT YOU APPEAR TO BE AFTER HERE IS A LOFT. *A LOFT.*

FILMS THAT ALMOST HAD GARAGES IN THEM

CITIZEN KANE

CASABLANCA (1942)

In the original draft of this all-time classic Humphrey Bogart's character rues that 'Of all the garages in all the towns in all the world, she walks into mine' after Ilsa surprises Rick while he is looking for a roll of brown string he could have sworn was in there somewhere. The studio later decided the film might be more interesting if Rick was a weary chap running a bar in Casablanca rather than a peevish man in Macclesfield who is trying to tie up a parcel of old shoes.

ZULU (1964)

The much-loved Michael Caine classic could have been very different if the first draft of the script had been adhered to, and in particular a legendary line which originally ran, 'Don't shoot 'til you see the contents of their garage'. Filming was in already in progress when the on-set historian pointed out that the Zulus didn't generally have garages. He also noted that the Anglo-Zulu War of 1879 didn't take place outside Reading. As a result, filming was moved to South Africa and the script was re-written with almost no references to garages at all, apart from at the very end, and three at the beginning.

INDIANA JONES AND THE TEMPLE OF DOOM (1984)

For the follow up to the acclaimed *Raiders Of The Lost Ark*, producer George Lucas decided to take things back to basics and pitched to director Steven Spielberg a work-in-progress script entitled *Indiana Jones and the Garage Of Things.* Spielberg immediately spotted several flaws with the idea, not least that Indiana Jones was unlikely to mistake a dust sheet draped over a broken child's bicycle for 'a scary ghost', nor would it take him almost two hours to walk around the garage before finding a magical stone underneath a bottle of turps. In the first instance, the legendary director suggested that the vague word 'things' be changed to something more dynamic like 'doom' and the rather limiting venue of a 'garage' become something a little more grand like a 'temple'. He also suggested that Lucas leave him alone to make a movie that wasn't 'total ass flakes'.

GARAGE SALE

These are the old sofa and spare tyre you're looking for.

SPACE GARAGE (1977)

As picked up by 20th Century Fox in the mid-'70s this classic film concerned a young man in a distant galaxy who was in the midst of clearing out his space garage so that there was room to park his small spaceship in it. In doing so, he enlists the help of various unusual characters including a tall, roaring bear-like creature whose enormous strength helps him to move an old bag of cement which has gone hard and fused to the floor. The studio later made a few suggestions as to how the script might be improved such as making it more about the fight between good and evil and not setting it in a garage at all. Also, they re-named it *Star Wars*.

THE SHAWSHANK REDEMPTION (1994)

The beloved tale of morality and friendship could have turned out very differently if it had followed the original plan to set it in a garage rather than a prison. It was only during pre-production that someone realised this gave relatively little scope for development of the relationship between the two central characters since, unlike a prison, criminals are not generally required to stay in a garage and would be free to wander off at any point. It was also highlighted that law-breakers are not generally put into a garage in the first place and that perhaps writer Frank Darabont had mistaken 'criminals' for 'carpet tiles'. Again.

BATMAN BEGINS (2005)

The smash hit franchise prequel could have been very different if it had been made as intended, telling the story of how Bruce Wayne originally came to be afraid of bats, how his parents were killed when he was a child, and how he set up a small business working out of a run-down garage on the outskirts of Gotham City, near the carpet showroom. Fortunately, just before filming began, it was realised that Bruce Wayne was the heir to a multi-billion dollar fortune and if he was going to set up a one-man business he could probably do it from a vast underground lair beneath his manor house. Also, it might be more interesting if the small business he set up was 'crime fighting' rather than, as originally intended, 'eBay shop selling novelty tea towels'.

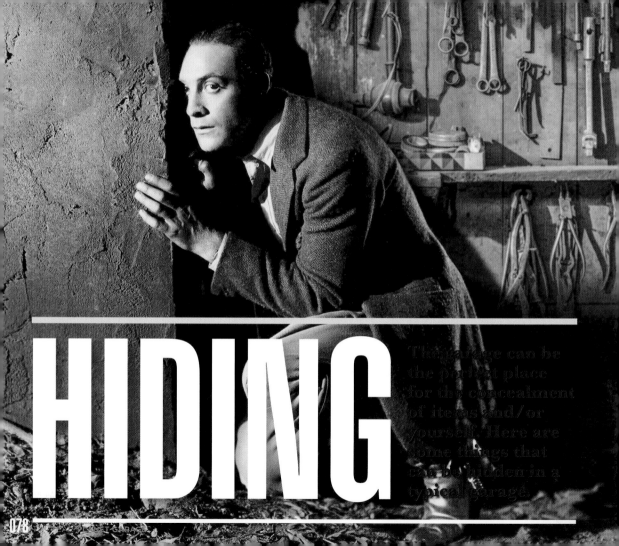

HIDING

The garage can be the perfect place for the concealment of items and/or yourself. Here are some things that can be hidden in a typical garage.

GENTLEMAN'S PUBLICATIONS

I f you have a small but much loved collection of nudey lady magazines, the garage could be the perfect place in which to conceal them. The garage could also be the perfect place to take a good look at yourself and ask what the flipping blimey you're doing with ancient soft pornography. It's not the 1970s you know. Although if it was, you shouldn't be hanging on to smut mags anyway, you should be dumping them in a hedge so that some weeks later gleeful teenagers can discover them.

AN ENORMOUS COLLECTION OF PORCELAIN OWLS

A garage is a perfect place in which to stash an enormous collection of porcelain owls. However, before doing so, ask yourself this: Do you run a market stall selling porcelain owls? Have you agreed to look after an over-stock of porcelain owls for someone who does? No? Then what are you doing with all the porcelain owls? Seriously, you might need help. Porcelain owl help.

THE PANDA

You still haven't managed to get rid of the bloody panda, but don't worry, the garage is still the best place for it. Just continue to lie about what else is in the garage – eg leaking flasks of nuclear waste, a crazed man with a knife, a very cross wolf – and longer term think about putting the panda behind some sort of false wall. Although you might want to ask the panda about this first. He or she might have some other suggestions, such as painting the back wall panda colours and agreeing to stand against it keeping extremely still whenever anyone else comes into the garage.

ACTUAL HIDING

Is this a playful game of hide and seek with your children? No? So you're actually hiding in the garage? This is all well and good, but is it really going to make your problems go away by concealing yourself indefinitely under a pile of dustsheets and old newspapers? For one thing, what are you going to eat? Just to be completely clear, this book has little-to-no nutritional content. Except the recipe section.

WHERE'S THE WALLY?

STORAGE

THINGS THAT CAN BE STORED IN A GARAGE

- Carpet offcuts
- Painty piece of wood
- White plastic garden furniture
- Old paint
- The lawnmower (unless massive and / or incapable of being turned off)
- Step ladder
- Statue of what might be Morrissey, inherited from mad aunt
- Jars
- Tools
- Screws
- String
- Geese
- A panda (short term)
- Your car

The garage excels as a place to store things. In fact, there's very little that can't be stored in a garage. Conversely, there are some things that very definitely cannot or should not be stored there. To make this clear, here is an handy guide.

▶ THINGS THAT PROBABLY CAN'T BE STORED IN A GARAGE

- A large passenger airliner
- A small passenger airliner
- Other sizes of passenger airliner – eg medium, tiny, sodding massive
- Fresh fruit
- Actual Morrissey
- An aircraft carrier (unless very, very small)
- A panda (long term, unless the panda is okay with it)
- Visiting Canadians

Finally, it's worth remembering that there is a fine line being 'storing' and 'hoarding'. If some television researchers arrive and tell you they want to make a programme about your 'storage', you may have a problem. Or just lots of interesting stuff. But probably the first thing.

Don't worry dear,
it's a quick fix...

MENDING THINGS

A rguably there is no greater use for a garage than as a place to mend things. That's why any right-thinking person will stock their garage with a selection of glues, along with an array of saws, hammers and pliers with which to remove the caps of the glues because they have dried up and sealed themselves in. The violent and perilous removal of the stuck cap from the glue is often more difficult and more time-consuming than the actual fixing of the broken item you set out to mend, which often takes only as long as the glue requires to set to your fingers and/or the newspaper you put down to stop it sticking to the surface beneath it.

Yeeeah - that's broken...

BREAKING THINGS
WHILE CLAIMING TO BE MENDING THEM

The garage is the perfect place in which to attempt a repair on something only to find you have actually made it worse. This can range from the simple, such as attempting to glue a sliver of china back into the edge of a plate only to drop the whole thing on the floor, to the more complicated, such as embarking on a mission to dismantle a mechanical device only to snap a small but quite vital part of the mechanism which will ensure that the thing never works ever again. Whatever the complexity of the task at hand, once you realise that you have royally knackered your chances of completing it, you must return to the house and announce with great confidence that the item in question was, sadly, 'unfixable'.

PART #3

CAR IMPROVEMENT

THE HOVERVAN

Owning a van is all well and good, but what if the area you live in floods? Then where are you going to be? Underwater, that's where. But not if you devote a little garage time to turning an ordinary van into an hovercraft. Here's how.

Owners Garage Manual

STEP 1

Drive your van into your garage.

STEP 2

Reverse your van out of the garage again. Retrieve the crushed and broken bicycles and the washing rack you forgot were in there. Hide them.

STEP 3

Drive the van back into the garage and begin by shedding unnecessary weight such as vast sections of the bodywork.

STEP 4

Remove the backdoors and fill the resultant hole with an massive fan connected to a high powered engine.

STEP 5

Attach a retractable skirt system to the perimeter of the van and cut a hole in the floor with another large fan poking through it, attached to another extremely powerful engine.

STEP 6

Head to a nearby lake or reservoir and drive straight into the water.

STEP 7

Sink.

Ah, yes, should have told you to turn on the fan engines. Not that it would have made much different. You're still basically driving a ruined van into a lake. Sorry.

OTHER USES FOR A GARAGE

As a setting for one of the crucial final scenes in which you discover that the guilty person was not who you suspected at all
At least, that's what they did in the first series of *Broadchurch*.

As a setting for an hilarious prank in which you build a very sturdy brick wall directly behind the door of your garage and then carefully paint it to look like the interior of your garage and then you leave the door open when your husband or wife is due home and they drive directly into what they think is the open garage but instead it's a very sturdy brick wall and they write off their car
No, wait, hang on a sec, that's not a good idea at all. What is WRONG with you?

As a tiny theatre in which you can re-enact scenes from once-popular police drama series *The Bill*
Bring joy to your neighbours, nay your whole town, by opening up your garage door every Friday evening to reveal a small stage and a backdrop of the infamous 'Jasmine Allen estate' against which you can perform classic scenes from old episodes of *The Bill*. Who wouldn't want to see someone in their garage shouting, 'Leave it aaaaaaht guv' and 'Watch it, I'm ex-job'. And who knows, perhaps you could get some actual ex-cast members of *The Bill* to join in. They're probably not that busy.

A SAUNA

A bit of pine, a hot steam-making thing, Bob's your uncle. They do it all the time in Scandinavia. That's why Volvos are designed to be left outside when it's minus 30; because everyone in Sweden has turned their garage into a sauna. Probably.

THE MOBILE GARAGE

The mobile garage has to be the dream for any right-thinking garage enthusiast. It's a garage, but you can take it with you. What's not to like? Apart from being at at home one day, realising that you need a screwdriver for something and then remembering that you've left the mobile garage lorry parked miles away. But on the plus side, you could be at a friend's house when they need a screwdriver and you'll be able to say with confidence, it's okay, I've got one in my garage, and return but two minutes later with the item in question, much to everyone else's amazement. Although your friends may have quite a few follow-up questions such as, 'Shouldn't you have an HGV licence to drive that thing?' and 'How can you afford this stuff; didn't you lose your job six months ago on account of your idiotic obsession with building a mobile garage?'

THINGS A GARAGE CAN'T

BE USED FOR

AN AIRPORT

Airports tend to be quite large. Garages aren't. Oh that's fine, you might say, I have a pretty long drive and then I'll open the garage door and the planes can drive in as they land. Wrong. The wings will get snapped off and then the airline will get very cross. Abandon this plan immediately.

AN AIRCRAFT CARRIER

Again, a terrible use of a garage. Aircraft carriers are enormous and require space on which to land advanced fighter aircraft. Oh yes, you might say, but my garage has a flat roof. This is almost certainly not enough. Also, and we cannot stress this enough, the primary requirement of an aircraft carrier is that it floats. Does your garage float? No, come on, answer honestly. You haven't even tried. This is not an encouragement to give it a go. Your idea is stupid.

A FLOATING AIRPORT

No, you see, that's an even worse idea. You're actually making this worse. You've basically just combined the two things we've just mentioned. Stop being silly.

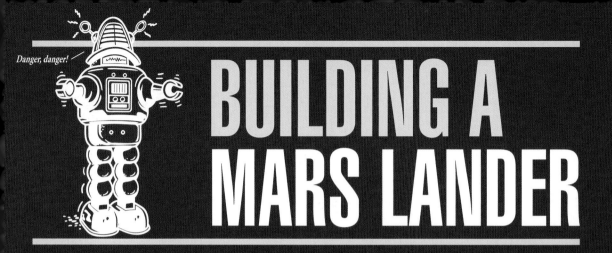

Danger, danger!

BUILDING A MARS LANDER

A recent study by the Office Of Fictional Statistics found that 'building a Mars lander' was one of the three most popular uses of a garage in Britain. If you've got a garage and you'd like to get in on this action, it's perfectly simple. Just follow the easy steps opposite.

GALACTIC GARAGE
MARS BASE ALPHA

1 Choose a colour for your Mars lander. WARNING: This is not as simple as it sounds. In fact, it is a highly complicated and technical process that must not be rushed.

RED - NO! Mars is also red. Your lander will blend into the surface and you will not be able to find it again.

ORANGE - NO! Didn't you hear us. Mars is red. An orange lander will clash.

BLACK - NO! It might look quite tasteful on the surface of Mars, but to get there your lander will have to pass through space, which is also black. Ergo, you won't be able to see it.

BLUE - Yes, possibly. But not turquoise. You don't want your lander to look too strident when it arrives on Mars.

WHITE - Classic. Your lander will look very snazzy when it arrives on Mars.

2 Build your Mars lander, launch it, let it land on the surface of Mars.

3 Job done!

WHAT SORT OF GARAGE DO YOU NEED?

1 WHAT DO YOU INTEND TO KEEP IN YOUR GARAGE?

a. Old paint cans, a stepladder, maybe a car
b. Erm... not a panda. No. Definitely not that.
c. Aeroplanes.

4 WHAT IS THE IDEAL SIZE OF YOUR GARAGE?

a. Two-car
b. Panda-sized
c. Airport-sized

2 **WHAT SORT OF FEATURES WOULD YOU LIKE WITHIN YOUR GARAGE?**
a. Shelves, power sockets, a cupboard maybe
b. Caging, bamboo storage, panda stuff
c. Check-in desks, shops, aeroplane parking

3 **WHO WILL BE GOING INTO YOUR GARAGE?**
a. Me, other members of my family, maybe my friend Neil who's come round to borrow a screwdriver.
b. No one. No one must find out.
c. Up to 50,000 passengers per day

5 **IF YOU HAD TO GIVE YOU GARAGE A NAME, WHAT WOULD YOU CALL IT?**
a. The garage
b. The pandatorium
c. Ipswich International Airport

YOUR IDEAL GARAGE IS...

MOSTLY A: Two-car, free-standing garage with a flat roof and a classic up-and-over metal door at the front. Perfect.

MOSTLY B: You've bought another panda haven't you? For God's sake Graham, this has got to stop.

MOSTLY C: What you appear to need is not a garage. It is an airport. The two are very different things. VERY different. For one thing, you probably need a licence for an airport.

THE OLD WARDROBE

For reasons that no one can quite explain, many garages have an old wardrobe at the back of them. What is it for? Who put it there? Well, it's a little known fact that the wardrobe at the back of the garage could carry huge significance. To find out if this is the case, go down to the garage in the middle of the night and slowly open the wardrobe doors. Now climb inside the wardrobe and close the doors behind you. Wait for a few hours. Have you been transported to a magical land beyond the back of the wardrobe? No? Are you, in fact, just sitting on a load of old shoes and some bottles of stuff that you think might be homemade beer from the 1980s? Well that's that one answered then. It's just a wardrobe.

THE
GARAGE
OF THE
FUTURE

In the future garages will look very different, what with computers and the internet and stuff. Here's what to expect from the garage of the future.

■ Highly advanced computerised child's bicycle (that is broken and has been under a dust sheet for five years now)

■ High tech, F1-style carbon fibre box containing random and unidentified screws, washers and Allen keys.

■ Full internets

■ Google-searchable cupboards.

■ Completely automated half-used paint-can-stacking robot

■ Doors that work off electricity or something.

■ State-of-the-art bag of old cement that's dried up and got stuck to the floor.

■ Endless ream of internet user comments just underneath the garage, largely made up of people moaning about the garage and being twattish to each other.

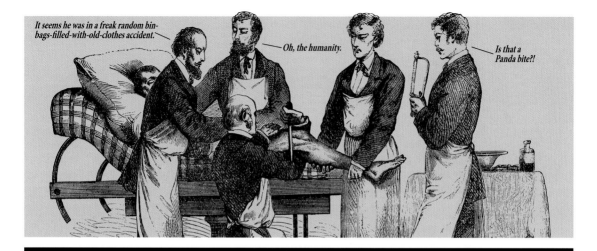

COMMON GARAGE INJURIES

Garages can seem like places of safety and sanctuary. Actually, the garage can be an extremely dangerous place. In fact, the British Council For Made-Up Statistics recently calculated that up to 42 per cent of all injuries happen in or near or within a 12 mile radius of a garage. Sobering stuff. Here are some of the most common injuries that can occur in a garage.

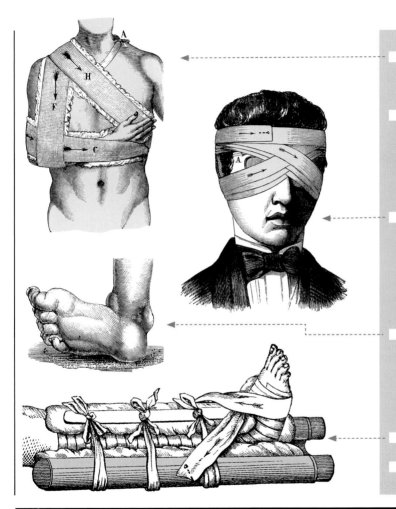

Crushed by automatic door whilst attempting to roll underneath it.

Getting run over by spouse who has forgotten that six months ago you turned the garage into a home office.

Buried by collapse of enormous pile of newspapers and magazines you've been meaning to take to the recycling centre since 2004.

Seeing what Peter has done to that screwdriver set he borrowed and becoming so furious that you kick something and break your toe.

Run over by Boeing 777.

Panda attack.

CAR IMPROVEMENT

TURNING YOUR CAR INTO A SNOWPLOUGH

Every year Britain is hit with a tiny flurry of snow and almost immediately everyone panics and drives their car into a ditch or stays at home while the news warns of TRAVEL CHAOS whilst people who grew up in Canada or Scandinavia laugh themselves stupid at the British inability to deal with anything except drizzle. Well, no more. If you've got a car and you've got a garage you've got all you need to turn your car into a snowplough*, just as *Top Gear* did with a combine harvester. Yeah. Here's how to do it.

Owners Garage Manual

STEP 1 Reverse your car into the garage.

STEP 2 Fit an enormous snow plough to the front, a flame thrower to the back and an urn of soup to the interior in case you get peckish and/or cold while you're out and about.

STEP 3

Drive around clearing roads / accidentally setting fire to cars / drinking soup. Simple!

STEP 4

Oh wait, you should probably check that the snow plough you're fitting doesn't make your car too wide to get out of the garage. We really should have mentioned that earlier. Sorry.

* Obviously you'll also need a heavy grade steel plough and various other materials, but let's not get bogged down in that.

THE WORD GARAGE IN OTHER LANGUAGES

- 🇫🇷 **French – Garage**
- 🇩🇪 **German – Garage**
- 🇮🇹 **Italian – Garage**
- 🇩🇰 **Danish – Garage**
- 🇳🇱 **Dutch – Garage**
- 🇸🇪 **Swedish – Garage**
- 🇷🇴 **Romanian – Garaj**
- 🇹🇷 **Turkish – Garaj**
- 🇺🇿 **Uzbek - Garaj**
- 🇪🇸 **Spanish – Garaje**
- 🏴󠁧󠁢󠁷󠁬󠁳󠁿 **Welsh – Garej**
- 🇦🇺 **Australian – Garage, mate**

GARAGE WEASEL REMOVAL

The garage weasel can be a terrible pest.
It eats your paint
It chews through newspapers
It can consume a small box of screws in seconds

BUT DON'T WORRY!

For just £200, we will visit your garage and remove all and any garage weasels that might be in there, giving YOU the peace of mind to use your garage to the fullest extent for whatever it is you're doing in there. Discretion guaranteed!

WESSOCKS

THE GARAGE WEASEL PEOPLE

AS FEATURED ON BBC WATCHDOG!

CLASSIC GARAGE BOOKS

CLASSIC GARAGE BOOKS

THE GREAT GARAGEBY
BY F. SCOTT FITZGERALD

Set in the heady times of the early 1920s, *The Great Garageby* revolves around a young man from out of town and a mysterious millionaire who owns the lavish garage next door into which he regularly invites guests so they can use his lathe and borrow his spanners. *The Great Garageby* is often celebrated as a fascinating depiction of its time, though it mostly gets bogged down with descriptions of tools and lathe settings which is why it was later re-written to be about people and New York apartments and such like. It's good, but it's not *The Complete Guide To The Garage* by F.G. Cockspode.

GARAGE 22 BY JOSEPH HELLER

A searing satire on the absurdity of garages, *Garage 22* uses a cast of bizarre, darkly comical characters to comment on many issues such as the redundancy of dust sheets and the folly of keeping touch-up paint for a car you sold several years ago. Brilliant in many ways, though not a patch on *The Complete Guide To The Garage* by F.G. Cockspode.

THE GARAGE OF WRATH
BY JOHN STEINBECK

Set during the Great Depression, this powerful work tells the story of a family forced from their home by circumstance and driven to live in a free-standing, double-doored garage. The 'wrath' in the title comes from the anger and in-fighting that results from being unable to find a small spirit level which was definitely in the garage somewhere and almost certainly on the shelf above the bench, if only someone would own up to moving it. A modern classic, although barely fit to lick the boots of *The Complete Guide To The Garage* by F.G. Cockspode.

GARAGE POTTER & THE PHILOSOPHER'S GARAGE
BY J.K. ROWLING

A young wizard begins to learn his craft at school when he hears of a mysterious garage which, so legend goes, contains an elixir of life. Young Garage Potter must find it before it falls into the hands of his enemies but his task is made harder by the state of the garage which is a right mess and has got a lot of old boxes and most of an Austin Princess in it. A ripping read, if nowhere near as exciting as *The Complete Guide To The Garage* by F.G. Cockspode.

ANIMAL GARAGE BY GEORGE ORWELL

A legendary political satire, *Animal Garage* tells the story of some farm animals who live in a garage. In one famous scene, they declare that all garages are equal, to the disgust of the humans who point out that most other garages are better than this one since most other garages don't stink of animal poo. A remarkable piece of writing, though a pale imitation of *The Complete Guide To The Garage* by F.G. Cockspode.

THE COMPLETE GUIDE TO THE GARAGE BY F.G. COCKSPODE

The holy text. If you've got a copy, hang on to it. It could be worth more than £4.

PART #6

CAR IMPROVEMENT

THE MOTORHOME

Many of us hanker after the freedom of owning a motorhome. Maybe you like staying in the middle of nowhere. Perhaps your idea of a good time is to defecate into a bucket. Whatever your reasons, you want a motorhome but you're not prepared to pay exorbitant motorhome prices. Nor do you want the responsibility of piloting a massive, unwieldy vehicle around narrow British lanes. No matter. Inspired by the plucky chaps on *Top Gear*, you can simply convert your existing car into a motorhome in the comfort of your own garage.

Owners Garage Manual

STEP 1

Reverse your car into the garage and get busy with the angle grinder, carefully removing the boot lid and some of the rear bodywork.

STEP 2

Around the enormous hole you have now made in the back of your car, construct a large tent-like structure which will form the fundamentals of your 'living space'.

STEP 3

Remove all the interior parts from the front seats backwards then put a mattress where the boot and back seat used to be.

STEP 4

Remove the dashboard cupholder and replace it with a camping stove. Hey presto, your 'kitchen area' is complete.

STEP 5

Ask the neighbours to water the plants and feed the cat because you're going on holiday!

STEP 6

Hotels are lovely places to stay, and often not as expensive as you might think. Probably should have mentioned that earlier. Sorry.

Films with **Garage** in the title

Produced & Released by

Company
NAME
PICTURES

THE GLADSTONE IN THE GARAGE (1951)

A whimsical Ealing comedy in which the people of Trimly idly gossip about local eccentric William Preesp who, it is rumoured, has a Gladstone bag in his garage containing something very unusual. After 47 minutes of this jaunty, harmless jocularity it turns out that what Preesp actually has in his garage is the embalmed corpse of 19th century British prime minister William Gladstone which he experiments on with abandon. After this revelation, the film takes on an altogether darker tone which saw it banned before release. In 1950s society its title was considered as shocking and unmentionable as words such as 'pantytrouser' and 'widdecombe'.

UP THE GARAGE! (1968)

A bawdy comedy in which jack-the-lad Sid Shagger (Sid James) engages in a variety of elaborate stunts in his attempts to get local nurse / stripper Babs Boobies (Barbara Windsor) to come into his garage to 'look at the plumbing'. Even by the standards of the day, *Up The Garage!* was criticised for its base humour and low quality double entendres, not least that one of main characters was called Peter Long-Penis.

GARAGE THRUST (1988)

Rick Toggle (Tom Cruise) is a top level-hot air balloon pilot who doesn't play by the rules. Lt. Dr. Sarah Sipovonoviczw is the no-nonsense Balloon Association safety officer who must tame him, and also sign off his balloon licence. Much of this movie takes place in Toggle's 'balloon workshop', which is the garage behind his house. For this reason, and also because hot air ballooning is extremely dull, this film was never released in the cinema or on VHS and was shown only on Air Canada internal flights for two weeks during 1991.

HARD GARAGE (1994)

Jean-Claude Van Damme plays Trent Hammer, a former Navy SEAL, astronaut and stuntman turned freelance pastry chef now working as a marine biologist on a remote island. When his estranged daughter Krystale falls in with a bad crowd of dolphin thieves, Hammer must prepare for what will be his toughest mission to date and decides to do so in his garage which has a multigym in it, and also a lot of guns. Described by *Completely Film* magazine as 'incomprehensible drivel'.

GARAGE (2002)

Liam Neeson plays tough retired CIA agent John Hardman who discovers his wife has been kidnapped and is about to be melted down. Immediately he heads to his garage to dig out all his old armour, weaponry and fake passports but the garage is rather a mess and he spends almost the entire rest of the film opening boxes, pulling out old shoes, CDs and a tea set, sighing, and then putting them back again. Production was beset with problems including the loss of the original garage location when the owner announced that he wanted to park his Austin Montego in it. Also, Neeson's performance was so breathy and low that his dialogue was incomprehensible and he sounded like a deflating canvas bag. As a result, the film was never released, although it was once given away free at Danish petrol stations.

PIRATES OF THE GARAGE (2008)

Cashing in on the trend for piratey films, *Pirates Of The Garage* tells the tale of a merry band of salty sea dogs who roam the oceans not in a tall sail-powered ship but in a garage (with sails on the top) and seek a bounty not of jewels and gold but of step ladders, old magazines and what was once the handtowel from the downstairs bathroom but has now been relegated to use as a rag for wiping oil off things. Speaking on BBC4's *Brains Trust* review programme, poet Tom Paulin described the film as 'startlingly shite'.

POTTERING ABOUT
JUST GOT DEADLY

LIAM NEESON

GARAGE

VEHICLES THAT AREN'T CARS

Cars aren't the only vehicles you can store in a garage.

THE BICYCLE

The bicycle is perfect for storing in your garage, especially since its compact size leaves plenty of room for other items such as discoloured garden furniture and a broken strimmer.

THE UNICYCLE

T On the plus side, a unicycle won't take up much room at all in your garage. On the downside, a unicycle is an idiotic way to get around, especially if there are hills involved. You do not need a unicycle unless your job description includes the word 'clown', and even then you could always use the comically small car that appears also to contain 17 other clowns.

THE RECUMBENT BICYCLE

This will take up more room than a normal bicycle. Also, when it's not in your garage it's probably out on the road with you riding it, and that means you look like a colossal ballbag. Honestly, what was wrong with a normal bicycle? But oh no, you have to make the point that you're so into cycling and so good at it that you can do it quite literally lying down. At least until you get run over by the lorry that didn't see you, you berk. The recumbent bicycle has no redeeming features, although if you threw it in a canal it might make quite a satisfying splash.

THE MOTORCYCLE

The great thing about a motorcycle in garage terms is that it takes up a lot less room than a car. In fact, in the space occupied by a car you could have three or four motorcycles. Although for the price of three or four motorcycles you could have just bought a car. Cars have heaters and don't get pushed over by local youths in the street. Worth remembering.

Could you turn up the air-con?

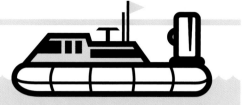

THE HOVERCRAFT

Keeping a hovercraft in your garage is all well and good but ask yourself this; how are you going to get it out again? You can't push it out because hovercraft don't work like that. All that'll happen is the underneath parts will get all scratched and you'll probably tear the skirts. No, to move it you're going to have to start it. And when you start it, everything else in your garage is going to get blown over and/or sucked into the hovercraft's vital working parts. Ergo, you haven't thought this through. And what in God's name are you doing with a hovercraft anyway? You live in Leeds.

THE LIGHT AIRCRAFT

Do you have a tape measure? Good. Go and measure the door on your garage. Once you've done that, go and measure the wingspan of your light aircraft. Is the first number at least a little big bigger than the second number? If the answer is no, this really isn't going to work. Also, how are you landing and taking off in that thing? On your street? Really? It's generally accepted that most runways aren't a cul-de-sac.

THE HEAVY AIRCRAFT

Honestly Simon, this obsession with turning the garage into an airport has GOT to stop.

WORRIED YOUR CAR WON'T FIT IN YOUR GARAGE? WORRY NO MORE WITH THE

BRISTLY CUMBERLAND
ACCORDIO-CAR SYSTEM

Our patented Accordio-car system simply removes the centre section of your car and replaces it with a massive accordion. Under normal driving your car remains the same length, but when you need to fit it into that tight garage, it simply shrinks in length until the door will close!

And our new *Mark IV* system uses electric motors, vastly reducing effort, time and grunting.

THE BRISTLY CUMBERLAND ACCORDIO-CAR SYSTEM

Make your car into an enormous accordion... today!

GARAGE
PRONUNCIATION
MAP

The word garage is pronounced differently depending on where in the UK you are. This handy map should help.

GA-RIJ

GAH-RAAAJE

INVENTING

COMPRESSED CHEESE
INVENTED BY:
ARTHUR KNEESBY OF MOOSE STOOL, INDIANA, USA. 1982
Like compressed air, but it's cheese. Completely pointless.

THE IRONY BOARD
INVENTED BY:
SHIELDA GROBE OF WAKEFIELD, UK. 1990
Actually made your clothes more wrinkled.

ILLUMOHAT
INVENTED BY:
RJOOST PATOOTOES, VOOSP, THE NETHERLANDS. 1994
Allow friends to find you in a crowd with this three metre tall illuminated hat. Stupid.

CAR MICROWAVE
INVENTED BY:
RANDY GRATTLE, TOMBOLA, ARIZONA, USA. 1989
Turn your car interior into a microwave. Pointless and quite insanely dangerous.

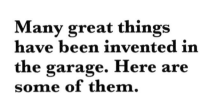

THINGS

Many great things have been invented in the garage. Here are some of them.

SMIRK ALARM

INVENTED BY:
PETR GNZZZ, ZIPTIE, POLAND. 2001

Activates a siren if anyone is smirking in your house. Pointless and very annoying, especially if you're Jack Nicholson.

SWISS ARMY TROUSERS

INVENTED BY:
HANS FREEKIT, BELM, SWITZERLAND. 1974

Trousers that can also be used as a jumper, a frying pan, a compass, a toothpick and many other things. Idiotic.

FACEBOOK

INVENTED BY:
LENDA CRACE, YAK SPIT, CANADA. 1999

A huge book full of pictures of people's faces. Surprisingly uninteresting.

DOG HATS

INVENTED BY:
ESTELLE RAPID, MALHEUREUSEMENT, FRANCE. 1969

Make your dog looks smarter with a hat. Completely stupid. Also, the dog didn't like the colour.

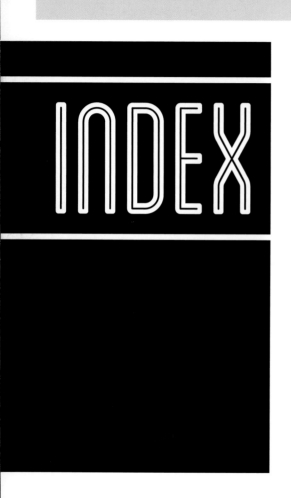